·Jane Goodall's·
ANIMAL WORLD

PANDAS

by Miriam Schlein

Scientific Consultant: Roger Caras

Collins

◇ Introduction: The Giant Panda by Jane Goodall

How exciting it would be to trek into the mountains of China where the last of the giant pandas live and see them in the wild. I have imagined sometimes what it would be like. Climbing the steep snow-covered mountainside through the bamboo forests, hearing a rustling in the undergrowth and then, peering intently and keeping very still, suddenly seeing a real, live giant panda looking back at you.

In fact I have only seen two giant pandas, and they, of course, were in zoos. One was the very famous Chi Chi. The other was her mate who was sent to London, on loan to see whether Chi Chi might get pregnant and produce a baby. Everyone was very interested in this marriage – but unfortunately it was not a success. Chi Chi and An'-An' got on very well, but they did not produce an infant. In fact, giant pandas are very difficult to breed in zoos, although today, because people know a bit more about them, some zoos have managed to breed a few.

The giant panda is so endangered in the wild, so beautiful, and so mysterious, that it has been adopted as the symbol for all vanishing wildlife by the World Wildlife Fund. We all know the little panda design that appears on all their literature. It was designed, originally, by the famous wildlife painter Sir Peter Scott.

At long last we know a little bit about how giant pandas live in the wild. For the very first time, Chinese and American field biologists have collaborated in order to study these animals in the bamboo forests. We all hope that the research will not only help us to understand giant pandas much better, but also help the Chinese government make and enforce laws that will give them and the bamboo forests where they live better protection. Otherwise the only giant pandas remaining will be those in zoos, and all the enchantment and magic of that wonderful creature in the wild will be gone. Our grandchildren will not be happy if we allow that to happen.

In this book you will find out more about this elusive animal. Perhaps some day, if you are very lucky, you will see a giant panda yourself.

◇ Contents

◇ Where Do Giant Pandas Live?

Giant pandas live high in the mountains of southwest China. They live there because that's where the bamboo grows, and bamboo is what pandas eat. In fact, the name "panda" means "bamboo eater" in Nepalese.

A few thousand years ago, the pandas lived in other parts of China. But the climate slowly got drier. And since bamboo grows best in damp areas, there was less bamboo. But in higher country, the air was moist and bamboo flourished. So the pandas went into the hills.

More recently, people began clearing those mountain foothills for farms. The bamboo was chopped down. So the pandas moved even higher, into the mountains. Now that is the only place where giant pandas live in the wild – high in the bamboo forests, 2,134 metres to 3,048 metres above sea level.

It's so high up, clouds drift through the trees. Many other un-usual animals live there too. There is the goatlike goral. The furry takin. There are rare golden monkeys and small muntjacs, or "barking deer". There are little whistling pikas that look like guinea pigs.

In winter, it is bitter cold. In spring it warms up. Wildflowers poke through the melting snow.

U.S.S.R.

MONGOLIA

CHINA

■**Distribution of giant panda**

Sichuan Province

Wolong Reserve

INDIA

BURMA

TAIWAN

Pacific Ocean

◇ The Family Tree of the Giant Panda

The Chinese name for the giant panda is *daxiong mao* (dah-shung-mah-oo) – "great bear-cat". The giant panda is certainly not a cat. But is it a kind of bear?

Some scientists say yes. It looks like a bear. It walks like a bear. Its cubs, when born, are very tiny – like a bear's. Its blood, when analyzed, is like a bear's.

Other scientists say no. They believe the giant panda is part of the raccoon family.

One of the special things about the giant panda is its unusual *panda's thumb* – sometimes called its false thumb. This is not actually a thumb, like humans have. It's part of the wristbone that sticks out to the side, like an extra, padded finger. The giant panda uses it like a thumb – to grasp things and pick them up.

Only one other animal, the red panda, has a panda's thumb. The red panda looks nothing like a giant panda. It looks more like a raccoon. It's small with a long, bushy tail, and is part of the raccoon family.

But the two pandas have other things in common besides the panda's thumb. The shape of their skull, teeth, and foot bones are more alike than those of the giant panda and the bear. The red panda is also a bamboo-eater. Since the giant panda shares so many basic qualities with the red panda, and since the red panda *is* in the raccoon family, it seems logical to place the giant panda in the raccoon family too. We know that the giant pandas have the same number of chromosomes in their cells as the raccoon – forty-two. Bears have either fifty-six or seventy-four chromosomes. Also, giant pandas don't hibernate, as bears do.

So, today, all scientists do not agree about the family tree of the giant panda. Some think it belongs with the raccoon. Some think it belongs with the bear. Still others think it is such an unusual animal it should be in a family by itself.

The scientific name of the giant panda is *Ailuropoda melanoleuca* (a-*law*-ruh-po-duh mel-*an*-o-loo-kuh), which means "black and white cat-foot". The scientific name of the red panda is *Ailurus fulgens* (a-*law*-rus *full*-jens), meaning "fire-coloured cat".

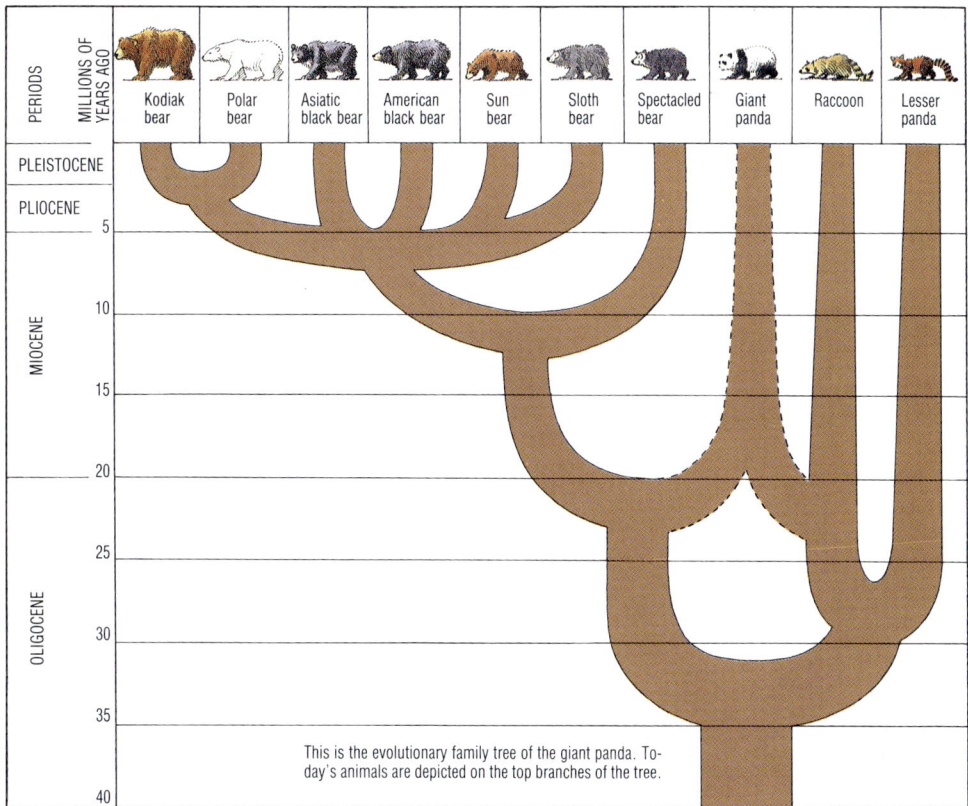

This is the evolutionary family tree of the giant panda. Today's animals are depicted on the top branches of the tree.

◇ The Giant Panda Community

Pandas don't live in groups the way many animals do, so we don't really think of them as living in a community. Each panda lives by itself, in its own special part of the forest called its *range*. A panda's range is only about four to ten square kilometres. Ranges overlap, so that one panda may share an area with several others. Still, each panda will spend most of its life alone.

Pandas do seek each other out in the spring, the breeding season. Then, male and female pandas wander into a neighbouring range looking for a mate. After the breeding season, the pandas quietly go their separate ways.

◇ Sizing Up the Giant Panda

The giant panda is really not such a giant. We just call it "giant" to separate it from the small red panda, which is sometimes called the lesser panda.

A male giant panda in the wild can weigh up to 109 kilograms. Females weigh a bit less – about 91 kilograms. The head-plus-body length of the giant panda is one-and-a-half metres at most.

Giant pandas in zoos get much heavier. This is because zoo pandas don't have much to do. They don't have to gather food. They don't have anywhere to go. They walk a bit. But most of the time they just lie around and gain weight.

After four years at the Moscow Zoo, Ping-Ping, a male panda, weighed 180 kilograms. After ten years at the Bronx Zoo, a female named Panduh weighed 172 kilograms.

Measurement: head-plus-body length

Grizzly bear
1.8–2.1 metres
(6–7 feet)

Lesser panda
0.6–0.8 metres
(2–2½ feet)

Kodiak bear
2.1–2.6 metres
(7–8½ feet)

Polar bear
2.1–3.4 metres
(7–11 feet)

Giant panda
1.2–1.5 metres
(4–5 feet)

Raccoon
43–56 centimetres
(17–22 inches)

9

◇ **How Giant Pandas Move**

The giant panda walks slowly, taking long, pigeon-toed steps. Its head sways from side to side. At its fastest, it might break into a clumsy trot. So a giant panda is not going to break any speed record.

But then again, it doesn't need to. For many animals, speed is what helps protect them from predators. The panda does have enemies in the forest, like leopards and wild dogs that hunt in packs. But many scientists think that an adult panda does not have to run to get away from them. With its strong jaws and big teeth, it can stand its ground and defend itself.

Giant pandas are also good tree-climbers. They grasp the trunk with all fours and shin up, bit by bit. Until they are big enough to defend themselves, young pandas can escape from danger by climbing trees. Adults will also climb trees to escape from wild dogs.

◇ The Senses of the Giant Panda

Pandas' eyes have long narrow pupils – the part of the eye that lets light in. Cats have pupils like this. The pupils give them good up-and-down vision, and are also better at controlling the amount of light admitted than round pupils like ours.

This suggests that pandas can see well in the dark. That would be useful, since they don't sleep throughout the night, but spend part of the night wandering about and eating.

Pandas also have a good sense of smell.

◇ How Giant Pandas Communicate

As we have seen, pandas normally live alone unless it is time to mate. But they do have ways of communicating. They can use their good sense of smell to detect messages from one another. One panda will rub its backside against a tree, leaving a sticky liquid there that another panda can smell. By sniffing this "message", another panda, who comes along later on, can tell that the first panda has been there, how long ago it was there, and whether it was a male or a female. This behaviour is called *scent-marking*. Many animals use this means of communication.

Giant pandas keep in touch through scent-marking all year long. But it is most important in the mating season, when the male and female pandas must find each other. Then pandas, who are normally very quiet, also communicate by making a lot of noise. To find each other, they yip, they bark, they even moo.

◇ Being Born

Male and female pandas mate only a few days during the year, some time between mid-March and mid-May. In late summer or early autumn, baby pandas are born. The mother panda finds a protected place – a hollow tree or a cave – and there she gives birth.

The baby is tiny and looks more like a mouse than a panda. Its pink little body has just a few white hairs on it.

Gently, the mother picks up the baby with her mouth. She holds it in her paws and licks it clean. Then she puts it against her breast so it can drink her milk.

As tiny as it is, the panda cub has a loud cry. When the mother goes out she carries the baby with her, carefully, in her mouth. If she left it alone, it would cry and attract predators. A panda mother gives a lot of care and attention to her baby.

◇ Growing Up

After a week, the baby panda begins to get its black and white markings. In a month, it's covered with fur and has a white face and black patches. Now it looks like a panda.

Five or six weeks go by before the baby's eyes open. At this point it starts to learn how to crawl. When the mother panda goes out, she still takes the baby along, but not in her mouth. Now she carries it in one forepaw and walks on three legs. After ten weeks, the baby panda can stand on its feet and take a few steps.

After this slow start, the cub grows quickly. In three months, it is sixty centimetres long and weighs about four-and-a-half kilograms. The mother panda plays with the baby a lot. She cuddles it. She lets it climb all over her. It likes to climb up on her back.

After about five months, the cub can trot alongside its mother. It starts to eat bamboo. But it continues to drink its mother's milk until it is eight or nine months old.

The young panda stays with its mother for about a year and a half. By then it weighs more than 45 kilograms. Then it leaves its mother to establish its own range and live the life of an adult panda. Pandas can live to be twenty-five to thirty years old.

◇ **Living Day to Day**

The panda is moving slowly through the two-metre high bamboo. Her black-and-white fur blends in with the shadows. If you were not very close, you would not even see her. Soon she stops to eat some bamboo.

Like monkeys and apes, the panda eats sitting down. She grabs a bamboo stalk, pulls it down, and bites it off. With her teeth,

she strips off the tough outside. Then, gripping it with her panda's thumb, she munches on the stalk, finishing it in less than a minute. Then she eats another . . . and another. After a while, she moves on. Later she will stop for another meal.

A panda eats more than 4,500 kilograms of food a year. This is almost 14 kilograms a day. In the spring when there are sweet young bamboo shoots, a panda will sometimes eat 36 kilograms of food in one day.

Pandas eat so much because they have intestines that are too short to digest bamboo properly. Animals that eat vegetation usually have longer guts. The panda's short "gut" is more like that of a carnivore – a meat-eater. In fact, the giant panda is descended from a carnivore that lived millions of years ago. Over time, the food supply changed, and there was less meat. But bamboo was plentiful, so the panda's ancestors got into the habit of eating bamboo. Yet as the panda evolved, its gut did not. Now it has a meat eater's gut, and a plant-eater's diet. And to get enough nourishment it must eat a lot.

Pandas still do like to eat meat

when it's available. Once in a while they catch a tiny pika, or a vole, or some other small mammal to eat. But that is not enough to live on. Even though the giant panda's diet is now about 99 per cent vegetation instead of meat, it is still classified as a carnivore. Pandas also eat flowers like crocuses and irises, which grow in their mountain habitat.

Day and night, pandas keep wandering and eating. When they get tired, they rest wherever they happen to be. They lean against a tree or lie down in the snow, and sleep a while. Usually they sleep for two to four hours, but sometimes for just a few minutes. Their thick oily fur keeps them warm and dry. Winter and summer, their routine is more or less the same.

◇ Giant Pandas in Captivity

The giant panda is a rare animal. There are fewer than 700 now living in the wild compared to, say, nearly one million zebras in Africa.

This is the reason that there are so few pandas in zoos. It is best to leave them in the wild. They have a better chance of surviving when left in their natural habitat.

Not many pandas have been born in zoos and lived. The first was in China, in 1963. Outside China, there were no births until 1981. Then, in the Chapultepec Zoo in Mexico City, a baby panda named Tohui was born. The first panda ever to be born and survive outside China, Tohui is still there, along with three more young ones also born at the zoo.

In 1988, there were about one hundred pandas in zoos and breeding centres in China, and fourteen in zoos in cities such as

London, Paris, Madrid, West Berlin, Tokyo, Mexico City, and Washington, D.C. These pandas were all gifts from the Chinese government.

Pandas in zoos are usually well cared for. The zoos are careful to provide trees to climb and pools to dip in. Some pandas in zoos have toys to play with – balls, barrels, and jungle gyms to climb. The bamboo that they eat must be flown in for them. Their indoor quarters are air-conditioned. This is essential for their health.

Although zoo life is not a natural life for a panda, they are kept as comfortable and healthy as possible. The zoo offers millions of people the chance to see these rare animals. In 1987, two pandas, Ling-Ling and Yong-Yong, visited the Bronx Zoo in New York for six months. About a million people came to see them.

◇ **Protecting the Giant Pandas**

There is a real danger that some day, maybe soon, there might be no more pandas in the world. They might become extinct. Gone forever. Can we keep this from happening?

The Chinese have led the fight to save the pandas. First, they set aside large areas as panda reserves. The reserves cover one and a half million acres. Then special laws were passed. Anyone killing a panda, even accidentally, gets a two-year jail sentence. Anyone who helps save a panda gets a large reward. Still, the number of pandas keeps dropping.

One big problem is their food supply. Bamboo grows in cycles – at regular intervals of from twenty to one hundred years, a particular bamboo species will flower. Then suddenly, every single plant of that species dies at the same time. This means that for about a year there is very little for pandas to eat.

There are three species of bamboo in panda country – umbrella, fountain, and arrow bamboo. In the 1970s and early 1980s, two of these had "die-offs". Over entire mountainsides, there was hardly any bamboo. During die-offs long ago, pandas would roam to where different types of bamboo still grew. But now, when they roam, they don't find bamboo. They often find farms and villages instead.

The pandas began to starve. Emergency food drops of yams and grain were made by helicopter. Rescue teams searched the mountains for starving pandas, carried them down, fed them, and kept then in holding areas till they were ready for release.

The World Wildlife Fund is an organization that helps endangered wildlife. This group is working with the Chinese government to help save the pandas.

In the Wolong Reserve, in Sichuan Province in central China, they set up a panda breeding station and research centre. Higher in the mountains some experts are studying pandas in the wild. The more we know of the habitats and the needs of pandas, the better chance we have of figuring out how we can save them.

One plan is to plant additional kinds of bamboo. Then, when one species dies out, the pandas can eat the others. Some experts think that the different reserves should be linked together. Then pandas could roam freely from one to the other if they need to, for breeding or food-finding. (Now the reserves are separated.) The cutting down of trees on reserves should also be stopped.

Scientists from many countries are helping in the panda project. Will it work? In years to come, will there still be pandas wandering through the forests?

We hope so.

About the Contributors

JANE GOODALL was born in London on April 3, 1934, and grew up in Bournemouth, on the south coast of England. In 1960, she began studying chimpanzees in the wild in Gombe, Tanzania. After receiving her doctorate in ethology at Cambridge University, Dr Goodall founded the Gombe Stream Research Centre for the study of chimpanzees and baboons. In 1977, she established the Jane Goodall Institute for Wildlife Research, Education and Conservation to promote animal research throughout the world. She has written three books for adults, including the bestseller *In the Shadow of Man*, and three books for children, including the recent *My Life With the Chimpanzees* and *The Chimpanzee Family Book*.

MIRIAM SCHLEIN is the author of more than 60 books for children. Six of those have been chosen as Junior Literary Guild selections, six others were named as Outstanding Science Books for Children, as selected by the National Science Teachers Association/Children's Book Council Joint Committee. She is the recipient of the Boys Clubs of America Junior Book Medal, and her book *Project Panda Watch* was cited as an Honor Book by the New York Academy of Sciences. She is the mother of two grown children and lives in New York City.

Jane Goodall's commitment to the animal world is expressed in her words, "Only when we understand can we care. Only when we care can we help. Only when we help shall they be saved." You can learn more about joining in her efforts to protect endangered wildlife by contacting The Jane Goodall Institute for Wildlife Research, Education, and Conservation, 1601 W. Anklam Road, Tucson, Arizona 85745.

First published in Great Britain 1990 by William Collins, Sons & Co. Ltd, 8 Grafton Street, London W1X 3LA.

First published in the United States 1990 by Atheneum.

Copyright © 1990 Byron Preiss Visual Publications Inc.

Introduction © 1990 Jane Goodall.

A CIP record for this book is available from the British Library.

ISBN 0 00 184588 8 (hardback)
0 00 184720 1 (paperback)

Printed and bound in Hong Kong by C&C Offset Printing Co. Ltd.

Cover photo copyright © by New York Zoological Society
Back cover photo copyright © by New China Pictures, Inc.
Front cover photo insert of Jane Goodall by Hugo Van Lawick, copyright © National Geographic Society
Introduction photo of Jane Goodall copyright © Ben Asen
Interior illustrations copyright © 1989 by Byron Preiss Visual Publications, Inc.

Interior photos: Pages 4, 8, 16, 20, 24, 26, 27 and 30 copyright © New China Pictures, Inc.; pages 1, 11, 25, 28, 29, and 31 copyright © Miriam Schlein; page 12 copyright © D. Demello/ New York Zoological Society; page 23 copyright © Bill Meng/ New York Zoological Society; pages 18 and 19 copyright © Pacific Press Service/Photo Researchers, Inc; page 14 copyright © Bo Hong Jin/Bruce Coleman, Inc.; page 10 copyright © Grace Davies/ Envision; page 21 copyright © Zig Leszczynski/Animals Animals.

Interior illustrations by Ralph Reese
Map by Rurick Tyler

Special thanks to Judy Wilson, Jonathan Lanman, Judy Johnson, Roger Caras, Bonnie Dalzell, Gao Xueyu, and New China Pictures, Inc.

Editor: Ruth Ashby
Associate Editor: Gwendolyn Smith
Cover design: Ted Mader & Associates
Interior design: Alex Jay/Studio J.

Ruth Thomas year 8 HB.